Written and Illustrated by Caroline Arnold

A Day and Night in the
DESERT

PICTURE WINDOW BOOKS
a capstone imprint

Tap-tap, tap-tap! Tap-tap, tap-tap!

It is an early spring morning in the Sonoran Desert. A woodpecker drills a hole in a saguaro [suh-WAHR-oh] cactus. The tall plant will be a good place to build a nest. On the ground below, a coyote looks for a shady place to rest.

A saguaro cactus can grow 40 to 60 feet (12–18 meters) tall. It is the tallest kind of cactus in the United States.

A jackrabbit spots the coyote and bounds away
on long, strong legs.

Shadows grow short in the midday sun. Heat bakes the desert floor. *Coo, coo!* calls a roadrunner. It races after a small lizard and catches it in its bill. The roadrunner runs back to its nest to feed its young.

A desert tortoise searches for flowers, leaves, and grasses. Its tough shell helps keep it cool. The tortoise breaks off plants with its mouth and chews them. When the tortoise is done eating, it goes back to its cool burrow.

A desert tortoise gets almost all the water it needs from its food. It can live without drinking for up to one year.

By afternoon the desert air is very hot. Most animals stay out of the sun. But the antelope ground squirrel does not seem to mind. It scampers across the desert floor, gathering seeds, fruit, and insects. Its tail shades its body like an umbrella.

The squirrel keeps watch for snakes and other predators. A red-tailed hawk circles in the sky. It is looking for something to eat. The squirrel sees the hawk and dashes to safety inside its burrow.

Antelope ground squirrels often climb barrel cacti to eat the fruit. No one knows how they keep from getting stuck by the cacti's sharp spines.

9

Daylight fades, and the desert air cools quickly. Nighttime animals come out to hunt and feed. Peccaries grunt to one another as they search for roots, fruit, and seeds. They use their noses like shovels to dig up cactus roots and other plants.

Peccaries are also called javelinas [have-uh-LEE-nuhs]. They live in groups, sometimes of more than 20 animals.

A prickly pear cactus hides the entrance to a pack
rat den. Its sharp thorns help protect the pack
rats from predators. Its fruit, when ripe, is a good
source of food too. Pack rats collect seeds, leaves,
cactus pads and spines, and store them in their den.

Stars twinkle in the clear desert sky. A ringtail climbs a cactus, looking for ripe fruit. Mice come out of their holes to collect seeds. A rattlesnake slips out from under a rock and gets ready to hunt. It can feel the ground vibrate when the mice move.

Whoo! Whoo! calls an owl. It searches on silent wings for rats, mice, and other small animals. It catches them with its sharp talons. The owl carries its prey back to its nest.

A rattlesnake injects venom into its prey through hollow, pointed teeth called fangs.

The cool midnight air is full of life. Bats swoop in the dark sky. Some chase tiny insects. Others drink nectar from cactus flowers.

A water hole in the desert
is called an oasis.

A-roo! A-roo! howls a coyote. All night long it hunts
for food. It will eat insects, lizards, mice, fruit, or
whatever it can find. When the coyote finds a water
hole, it stops for a drink. Scorpions and tarantulas
crawl nearby, looking for spiders and insects to eat.

All through the night, desert animals are busy looking for food. A kangaroo rat finds some seeds and stuffs them into pouches in its cheeks. It will store the seeds in its burrow.

A kangaroo rat has long hind legs. It can leap several feet in one hop.

A kit fox looks and listens for rats and mice. Its large ears can hear their tiny, high-pitched sounds. The kit fox sees a kangaroo rat and pounces. But just in time, the kangaroo rat leaps away to safety.

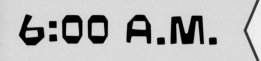

The sky grows light, and the sun peeks over the horizon. Nighttime animals settle down for the day. Owls return to their nests, the kit fox goes to its burrow, and the peccaries curl up for a nap. It is time for daytime animals to wake up and start a new day. Lizards warm themselves, jackrabbits find leaves to nibble, and birds collect food for their young.

Every day and every night, animals find food, water, and safe places to rest in the desert. It provides them with everything they need.

What Is a Desert?

A desert is a dry place. It gets less than 10 inches (25 centimeters) of rain a year. There are four major deserts in North America: the Great Basin, the Mojave [muh-HAHV-ee], the Chihuahuan [chee-WA-wan], and the Sonoran.

The Sonoran Desert covers parts of Arizona, California, and the Mexican states of Baja California and Sonora. In summer, daytime temperatures can reach higher than 110 degrees Fahrenheit (43 degrees Celsius). In winter, nighttime temperatures can drop below freezing. Plants and animals that live in the Sonoran Desert are adapted to its extreme climate.

Throughout the day and night, animals are busy in the desert. Diurnal animals are active during the day. Nocturnal animals are active at night. Which animals in this book are diurnal? Which are nocturnal? Where do they live in the desert?

Where Can You Find Deserts?

Deserts are found all around the world. Some are hot. Others are cold. The largest desert in the world is the Sahara Desert, in Africa. It covers more than 3 million square miles (7.8 million square kilometers). Only about one-fifth of the world's deserts are sandy. Most deserts, including those in the United States, are rocky or mountainous.

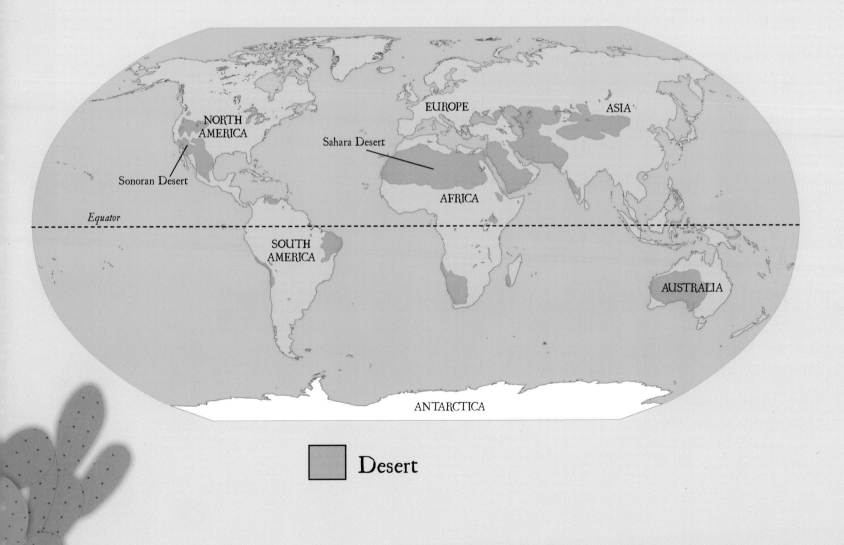

NORTH AMERICA

Sonoran Desert

EUROPE

ASIA

Sahara Desert

AFRICA

Equator

SOUTH AMERICA

AUSTRALIA

ANTARCTICA

Desert

Fun Facts

- A jackrabbit's large ears help it stay cool. Blood flowing through the ears allows extra body heat to pass into the outside air.

- The Gila monster is the only venomous lizard in the United States. Its bright colors warn predators to stay away.

- Thick coats protect bighorn sheep from the hot desert sun during the day. They keep the sheep warm at night.

- Desert tortoises dig shallow holes in the ground. When it rains the holes fill with water for the tortoises to drink.

- A roadrunner doesn't usually fly, but it is a speedy runner. It can run up to 20 miles (32 kilometers) per hour as it chases prey.

- When peccaries sense danger, they cough loudly and produce a smelly odor. To defend themselves from predators, they use their knife-like tusks.

- Scorpions often bury themselves in sand to avoid the hot sun. The scorpion's hard outer shell helps keep moisture inside its body.

- Stiff tufts of hair protect the bottoms of a kit fox's feet from the hot desert ground.

Critical Thinking Using the Common Core

1. Describe how the passing of time is shown throughout this book. (Integration of Knowledge and Ideas)

2. Name three diurnal predators in the Sonoran Desert and their prey. Then name three nocturnal predators and their prey. (Key Ideas and Details)

Glossary

adapt—to change to fit into a new or different environment

burrow—a tunnel or hole in the ground made or used by an animal for shelter

cactus pad—the flat, paddle-shaped stem of certain cacti, such as the prickly pear

climate—average weather of a place throughout the year

diurnal—active during the day

habitat—the natural home or environment of an animal, plant, or other living thing

horizon—the line where the sky and the earth or sea seem to meet

inject—to put into

nectar—a sweet liquid found in many flowers

nocturnal—active at night

predator—an animal that hunts other animals for food

prey—an animal hunted by another animal for food

talon—a long, sharp claw of a bird

venomous—full of venom, a poison injected into a victim by biting or stinging

vibrate—to move back and forth quickly

Read More

Anderson, Sheila. *What Can Live in a Desert?* Animal Adaptations. Minneapolis: Lerner Publications, 2011.

Pattison, Darcy. *Desert Baths.* Mt. Pleasant, S.C.: Sylvan Dell Pub., 2012.

Rissman, Rebecca. *Living and Nonliving in the Desert.* Is It Living or Nonliving? Chicago: Capstone Raintree, 2014.

Slade, Suzanne. *What Eats What in a Desert Food Chain?* Food Chains. North Mankato, Minn.: Picture Window Books, 2013.

Index

Internet Sites

FactHound offers a safe, fun way to find Internet sites related to this book. All of the sites on FactHound have been researched by our staff.

Here's all you do:

Visit *www.facthound.com*

Type in this code: 9781479560721

Check out projects, games and lots more at
www.capstonekids.com

Thanks to our advisers for their expertise, research, and advice:

Cecil R. Schwalbe, PhD, Wildlife and Fisheries Program
University of Arizona, Tucson

Terry Flaherty, PhD, Professor of English
Minnesota State University, Mankato

Editor: Jill Kalz
Designer: Lori Bye
Art Director: Nathan Gassman
Production Specialist: Kathy McColley
The illustrations in this book were created with cut paper.
Design Elements: Shutterstock/Alfondo de Tomas (map),
    Alvaro Cabrera Jimenez

Picture Window Books are published by Capstone,
1710 Roe Crest Drive, North Mankato, Minnesota 56003
www.capstonepub.com

Library of Congress Cataloging-in-Publication Data
Arnold, Caroline, author, illustrator.
  A day and night in the desert / written and illustrated by Caroline Arnold.
      pages cm.—(Nonfiction picture books. Caroline Arnold's habitats)
  Summary: "Highlights the activities of animals in the Sonoran Desert during one average 24-hour period"—Provided by publisher.
  Audience: K to grade 3.
  Includes bibliographical references and index.
  ISBN 978-1-4795-6072-1 (library binding)
  ISBN 978-1-4795-6084-4 (paperback)
  ISBN 978-1-4795-6144-5 (eBook PDF)
1. Desert animals—Behavior—Juvenile literature. 2. Desert animals—Juvenile literature. 3. Sonoran Desert—Juvenile literature. I. Title
  QL116.A74 2015
  591.754 2 23   2014025333

Look for all the books in the series:

Printed in the United States of America in North Mankato, Minnesota   092014   008482CGS15